D1504606

Table of Contents

What You Will Need

crayons

eraser

colored
pencils

markers

pencil

Cartooning for Kids!

Silly Sports

By Dave Garbot

Publisher: Rebecca J. Razo

Creative Director: Shelley Baugh

Production Director: Yuhong Guo

Senior Editor: Stephanie Meissner

Managing Editor: Karen Julian

Developmental Editor: Janessa Osle

Editorial Assistant: Julie Chapa

Production Designer: Debbie Aiken

Illustrated and written by Dave Garbot

www.walterfoster.com

6 Orchard Road, Suite 100

Lake Forest, CA 92630

Printed in China

February 2015

1 3 5 7 9 10 8 6 4 2

19265

Drawing paper

Getting Started

Do you like to play football, basketball, or baseball? Maybe you like to ice skate, run, or even snowboard. Many people enjoy sports and sometimes play more than one! Whatever you like to do, the most important thing is to have fun. In this book, we'll take some favorite sports and learn to draw the characters that play them, but with a little extra silliness too! On your mark, get set...draw!

Silly Features

Here are a few things you can use when drawing your characters. Maybe you'll want a curly hairdo, crazy eyeballs, or a bushy beard for your sports hero! It's all up to you. Come back to these pages anytime you need some ideas.

Accessories

Some of the items on the next page don't exactly look like the objects you would normally need when playing a game, but these are "silly" sports after all, and anything goes! Come back to page 11 anytime you need an idea or you're looking to add some extra fun to your drawing.

Section One

Contact Sports

When playing contact sports, you're allowed to touch, bump, and even knock over the other players! Yikes! Don't worry, it's all just part of the game. These players need extra equipment to protect them from getting hurt. Have fun, but don't forget your helmet!

Football Freddie

This guy is one tough cookie—and he also loves cookies.
Draw him holding a cookie—or maybe a few!

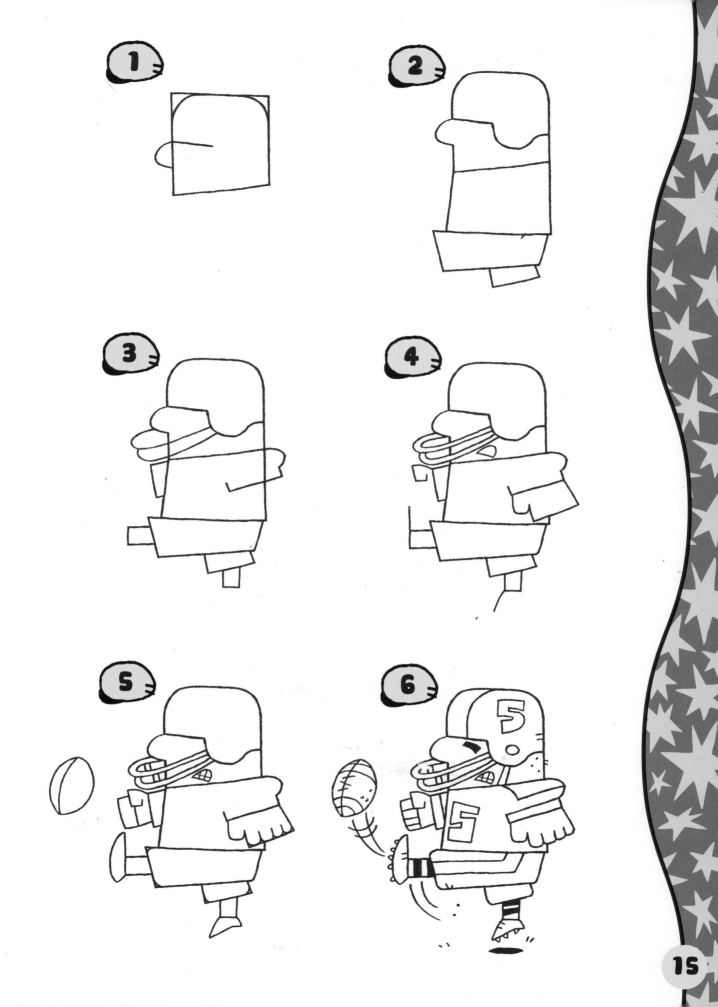

Soccer Susie

Can you give Susie a different kind of ball to kick?
If she kicks the ball forward instead of back over her head,
how would you draw her eyes?

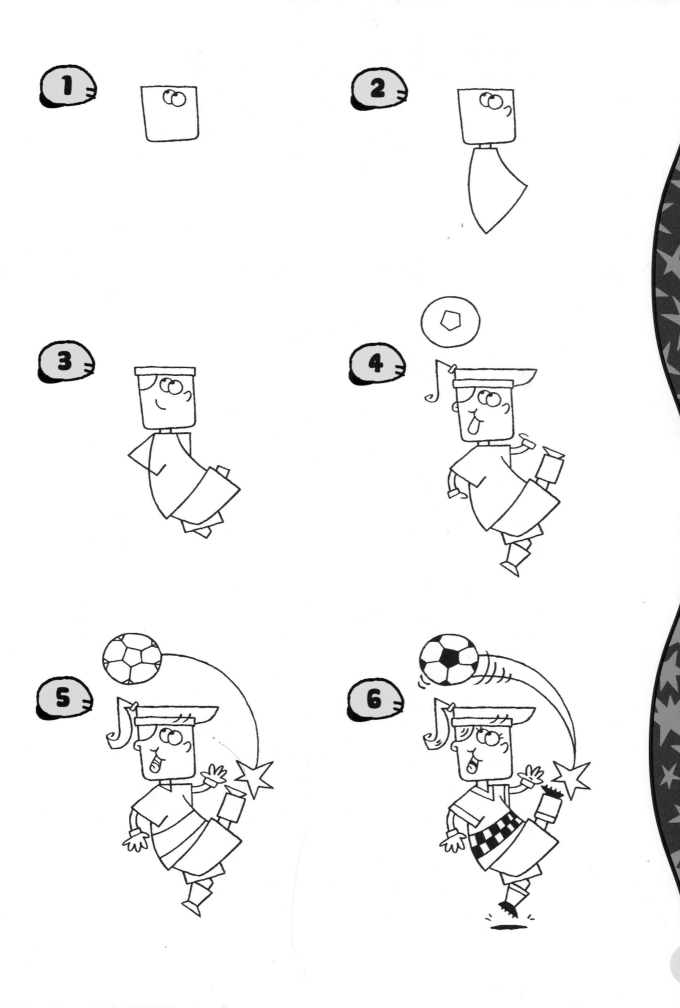

Hockey Hans

Hans looks unhappy. Can you give him a smile instead?
How about a smile for the bird on his uniform too?

19

Basketball Billy

Can you draw this player dribbling both balls at the same time? What else can you change? When you're finished drawing one player, try drawing the entire team!

Karate Ken

How would Karate Ken look with a silly hat instead of a headband? once you've drawn this master, try drawing an opponent to face him!

LaCrosse Larry

Lacrosse is played with special sticks.
What if you gave this player a mop instead?

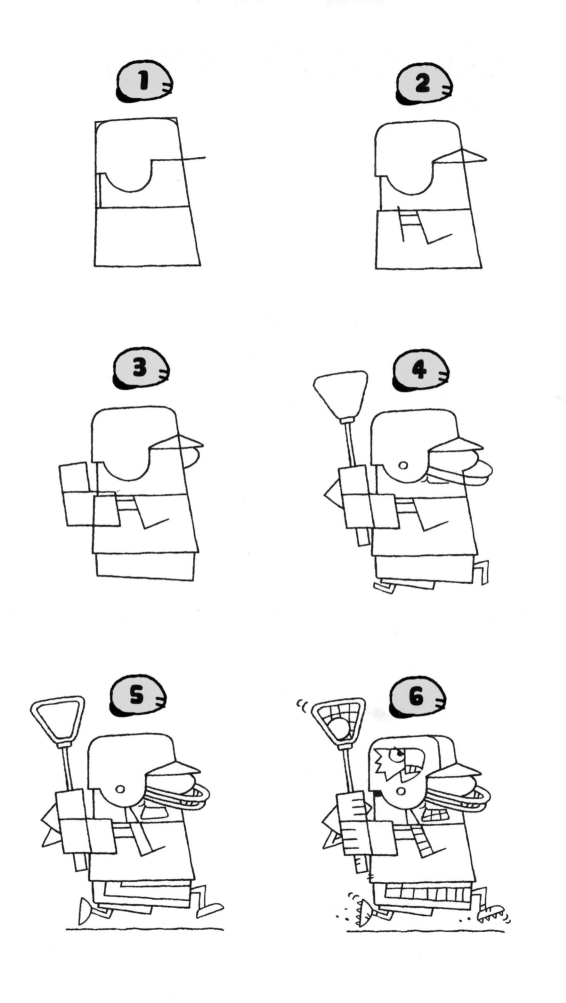

Roller Derby Debbie

This tough roller gal looks a little wobbly. Try drawing her with both skates on the ground.

Traditional Sports

Traditional sports are games and activities that you can play with a team or sometimes even by yourself. Whatever the case may be, it's fun to play, and extra silliness in this section is always a possibility!

Ice Skating Sally

Can you draw Sally with her eyes open? How about with a different hat and mittens? If you draw the groundline a little lower, it will look as if she's jumping in the air!

Gymnast Gemma

Do you think Gemma could balance something on her head while she performs? How about a bird, a plant, or a bunny? When you're done, try drawing Gemma in a different pose.

Golfing Greg

This golfer would look even sillier if the head of his club were gigantic! Try making it bigger or even smaller!

Tennis Tim

Did you ever see a square tennis racket? Change the shape and see how it looks! Instead of a visor, you could give your player a headband. How would that change the rest of your drawing?

Archer Archie

What if you replaced the arrow with something silly?
Go back to page 11 if you need an idea.

Baseball Bobby

Can you draw this player catching something else?
How about an apple or a taco?

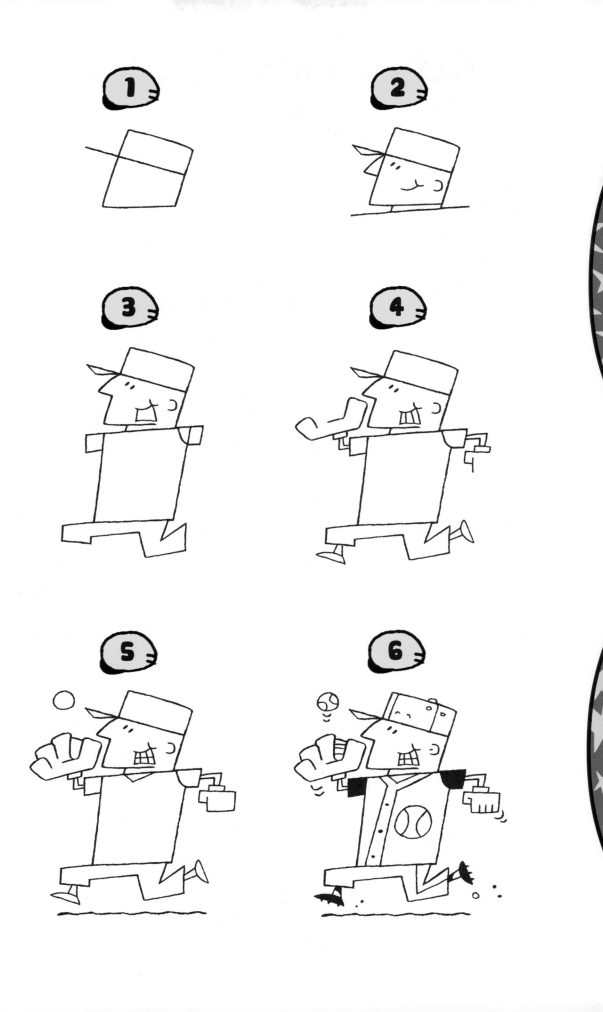

Fencing Ferdinand

En garde! Can you give this fencer a silly hat?
He's way too serious.

On Land & In Water

Some sports can only be played in the water, while others are only played in the snow! The characters in this section need some special accessories to play their games and keep things a little goofy too! So keep your bathing suit and mittens handy...you might need them!

45

Bicycling Betty

That is a crazy-looking helmet. How about adding some fancy ribbons to the bike handles to really make her fly!

Fishing Frank

Can you add one or two birds on top of Frank's hat?
How about more fish in the water too?
Fish love cookies!

Kayaking Katie

Can you add a few fish to this scene?
How about more birds?

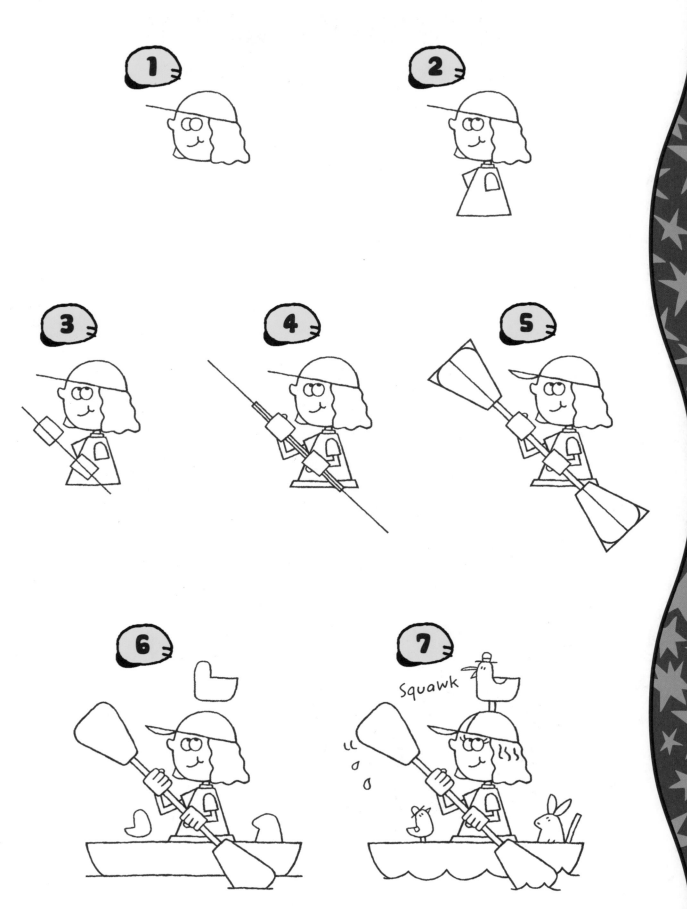

Scuba Diving Steve

These fish love ice cream! Can you give this diver another cone in his other hand? How about two scoops?

Surfing Sunny

How about adding some groovy shades to these surfer dudes?

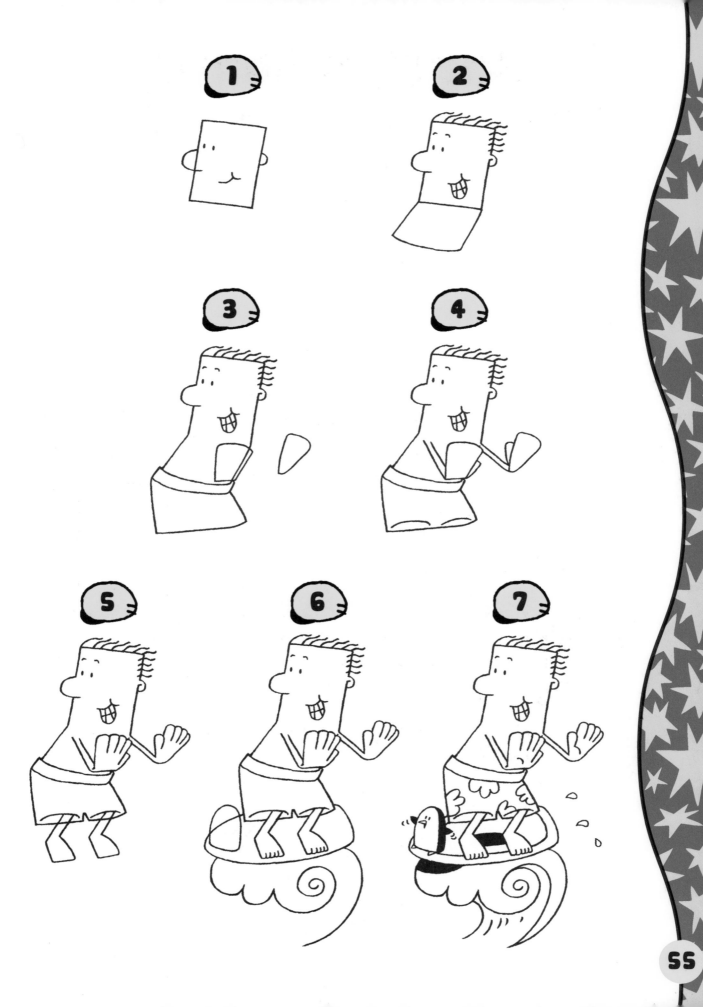

Car Racing Robbie

Can you add a cool design to this racer's car and helmet?
Adding the groundline below the wheels and little puffs of
dust and rocks in the last step will make your racer look
like he's really moving!

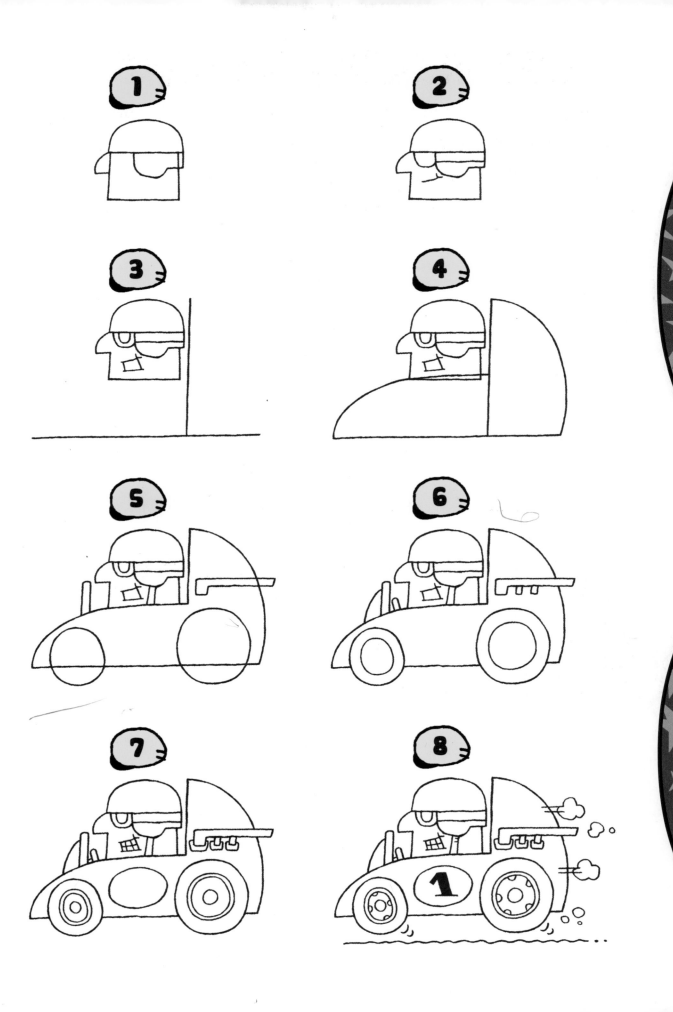

Snowboarding Spike

Snowboarders like wild hats and board designs. Can you change Spike's hat and board design to something really crazy?

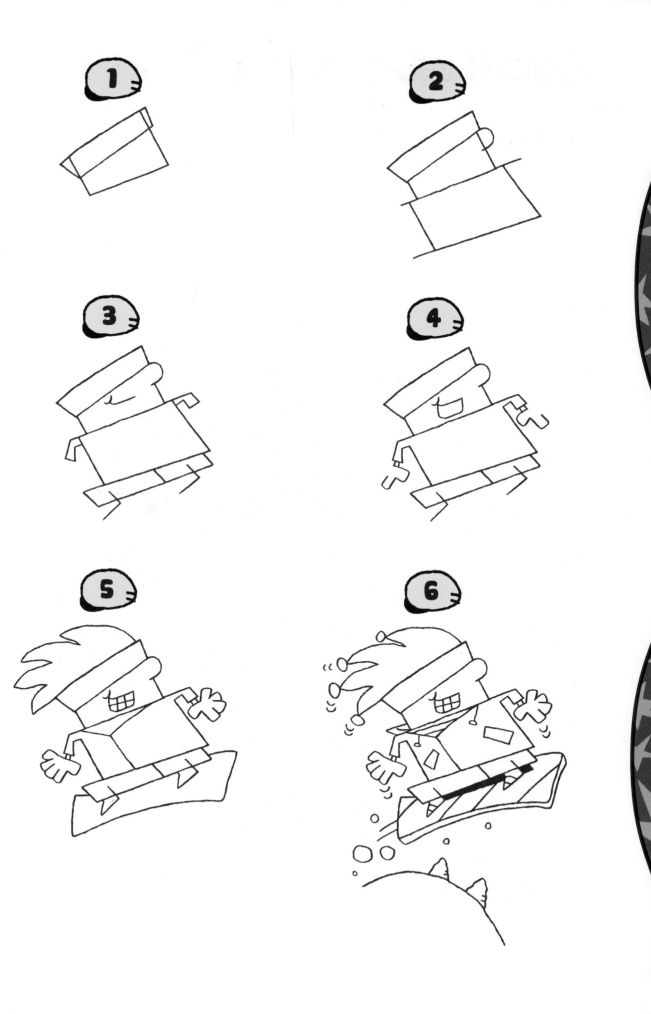

Skiing Sara

How would this skier look without her poles? Can you change anything else? Tilting the shapes slightly will make her look like she's going downhill!

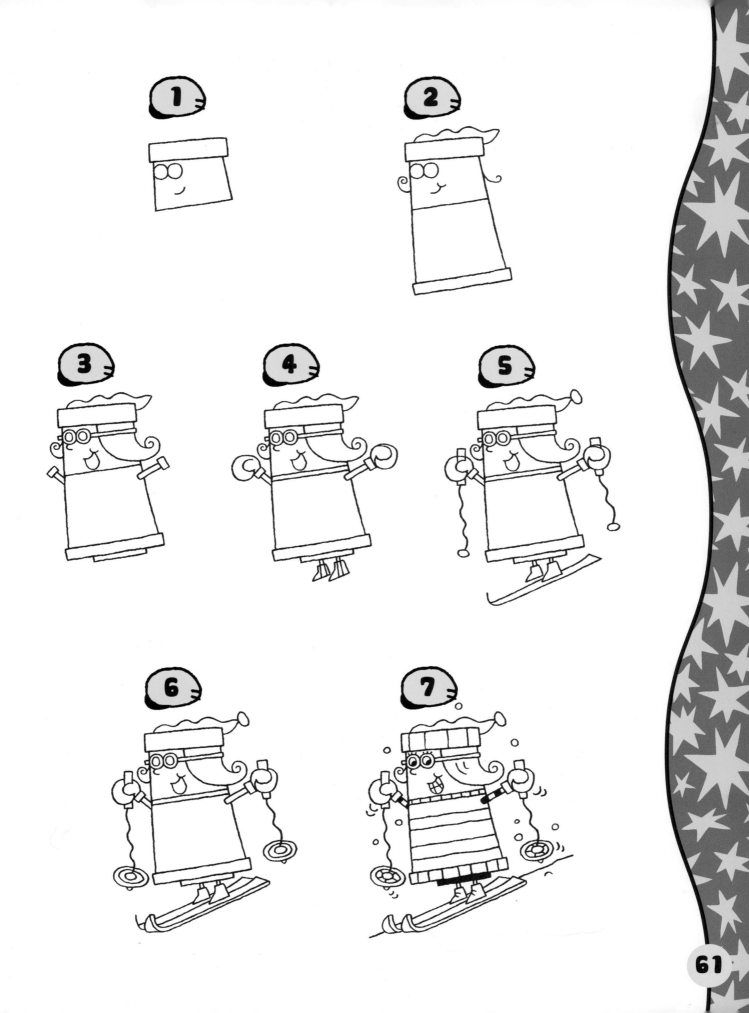

Running Randy

This track star might look pretty silly with fluffy slippers on his feet! Once you draw one runner, draw another one, two, or maybe even five more behind him to make it a big race!

About the Author

Dave Garbot is a professional illustrator and has been drawing for as long as he can remember. He is frequently called upon to create characters for children's books and other publications. Dave always has a sketchbook with him, and he gets many of his ideas from the things he observes every day, as well as from lots of colorful childhood memories. Although he admits that creating characters brings him personal enjoyment, making his audience smile, feel good, and maybe even giggle is what really makes his day.

Dave is from Portland, Oregon, and you can see more of his work at www.garbot.com.